# Indian Remains In Southern Georgia: Address Delivered Before The Georgia Historical Society

## Charles Colcock Jones

In the interest of creating a more extensive selection of rare historical book reprints, we have chosen to reproduce this title even though it may possibly have occasional imperfections such as missing and blurred pages, missing text, poor pictures, markings, dark backgrounds and other reproduction issues beyond our control. Because this work is culturally important, we have made it available as a part of our commitment to protecting, preserving and promoting the world's literature. Thank you for your understanding.

INDIAN REMAINS IN SOUTHERN GEORGIA.

# ADDRESS

DELIVERED BEFORE THE

# Georgia Historical Society,

ON ITS

TWENTIETH ANNIVERSARY,

February 12th, 1859,

BY

CHARLES C. JONES, Jr.

Savannah:
STEAM PRESS OF JOHN M. COOPER & CO.
1859

# Address.

When Wilkie was in the Escurial, looking at Titian's famous picture of "The Last Supper," an old Jeronymite said to him: I have sat daily in sight of that painting for now nearly three-score years. During that time, my companions have dropped off one after another; all who were my seniors, all who were my cotemporaries—and many, or most of those who were younger than myself. More than one generation has passed away, and there the figures in that picture have remained unchanged. I look at them until I sometimes think, *that they are the realities, and we but the shadows.*

This experience of the old Jeronymite, is but an individual confirmation of a truth sustained by every fact in history. States and empires wax in all the pride and pomp of population, conquest and wealth—and waning, oft times bequeath to succeeding generations only an occasional name—a broken fragment—to redeem the race and the age from total oblivion.

Were now is the temple of Belus, with its colossal statues of pure gold? Where the massive walls, the royal palace, the beautiful hanging gardens? Where now is he, proud monarch of Babylon, who claimed for himself and the splendid monuments of his genius, and exhaustless riches—an immortality which the ravages of time could not impair? A mightier conqueror than even he, has levelled all his greatness with the dust, and that matchless King whose fame once filled to its utmost confines the known world—his warriors dead, his princely merchants and cunning artizans forgotten, his treasures scattered, his solemn temples mingled with the silent dust, now sleeps in a nameless tomb.

Even the vast pyramid fails alike to rescue the mortal remains, as well as the reputation of the Egyptian king, from utter forgetfulness. An earthquake in one short moment, destroyed the pride of Rhodes. The Son of Saturn and Rhea, whom Phidias caused to descend from his celestial throne, has become the prey of time and virtuosi, who rival each other in the work of havock and spoliation. The works of the age of Pericles, lie at the foot of the Acropolis in indiscriminate ruin. The plough-share reveals the marble which the hands of Phidias had chiseled into beauty, and the shepherd folds his flocks beneath the falling columns of the temple of Minerva.

If even the adytum of the Egyptian temple has thus been robbed of its pristine sanctity, and has become the hiding place of the bat, while the wild winds of Heaven rave madly in the ruined "Hall of the Zodiac"—if the Persian column no longer graces the plain from which it sprang—if the wild moss and the untrained ivy have over-shadowed the classic honey suckle, the Persepolitan water-leaf, and the crisp Acanthus of Attica—if even the Minerva of Phidias, and the temples of Cimon are scarce remembered—if the children of the Graces, and the sons of Mars, who once filled the world with trophies of Art, and the splendors of warlike glory, live only upon the pages of history, "the wonder of an hour"—can it be a matter of surprise, that the poor unlettered Indian, and the few frail specimens of his rude arts, should have silently and unnoticed, faded from the remembrance of succeeding generations?

Of the three great instruments of civilization, without a knowledge and use of which no nation can ever achieve any material advancement, or give to humanity any assurance of its greatness, to wit: *iron*, the indispensable instrument of husbandry, and the beginning of all art,—*money*, the invisible bond that unites all civilized nations, however remote, and *alphabetical writing*, that places existing generations in communication with the past and the future—the Indians of Southern Georgia were entirely ignorant.

It was the lamentation of the old chieftain at Mucclasse, that the white man had not sooner come among the children of the forest, to furnish them with, and to teach them the use of letters, of the iron hatchet, the knife, the hoe, and the gun.

Without a knowledge of these three powerful primary instruments, by which are conferred the rudiments of all further advancement in civilization, and without the assistance of which no permanent or memorable monument of art can ever be achieved, it excites no wonder that the Indian of our region should have disappeared, leaving scarce a vestige to remind us of the fact, that upon these very plains now so replete with the products of intelligent industry, another, and a far different race once lived, loved, sported, warred, and died. The rude bark no longer tells the story of the battle,—upon the bright waters of our rivers and inlets are no more reflected the images of their graceful canoes—the deep forests give back no more the hunters call, or the echoing war-whoop of the brave, and from the softly breathing winds of evening, we can gather no tales of the loves of the wooing and the wooed.

There can be but little in the history of the hunter-state of man, that may be dignified with the name of monuments—little that can for centuries' with-stand the powerful influence of inherent decay and obscuration. In the language of Dr. Schoolcraft: "tribes who rely on the bow and arrow for their means of subsistence, who cultivate the earth by loosening the soil with the scapula of a stag or a bison, who are completely erratic in their habits and customs, and who erect as a shelter from the inclement elements, buildings of the slightest and most perishable materials, cannot be expected to have left very extensive or striking monumental traces of their past history. To waylay an enemy, to shake his scalp in the air, to follow successfully the tracks of the deer, to brandish the war-club in the dance, these were esteemed greater achievements among them, than to erect a column, or inscribe a shaft.

And yet they have not passed away without a mark.

Their sweet native language is linked with our Rivers and Mountains, our Valleys and Waterfalls. Long after the graves of their Chieftains shall have been levelled with the plain;—when the plough-share will no more reveal the stone which they had chiselled into use and symmetry, these names will perpetuate the memory, and hallow the recollection of those who first beheld and admired their beauties.

Among the scattered remains which still exist, are seen no fluted columns, no piles of solid masonry, no "gates of rust coated brass,"—no splendid ruins, no specimens of antique art, redolent still of the chaste imagination and cultivated taste that invested them with such exquisite symmetry and fair proportion, will reward the industrious investigator. The Indian alone appears before us, in the native simplicity of his manners, customs and utensils.

> "Let not ambition mock their useful toil,
> Their homely joys, and destiny obscure;
> Nor grandeur hear with a disdainful smile,
> The short and simple annals of the poor."

Rather let a generous interest be felt and manifested in the collection, arrangement, and preservation of every memorial and decaying memento of the race; for these will furnish us, as a Society, with interesting facts and useful information, connected with the early history and antiquities of our State.

With those anomalous ruins, that indicate in far distant periods, the existence of a race superior in point of civilization, and prior in point of time to the Indians who here inhabited, when Georgia was first settled by the whites, we have at present no concern—nor are we now permitted a discussion of those questions, suggested by an inquiry into the origin of the race. We cannot now attempt an estimate of the mental type and intellectual capacity of the Indian. A history of their manners and customs, the theory of their religious belief, are also foreign to our purpose, which is simply to present a brief notice of the few lingering traces of the Indians, which, after the lapse of certainly not less than a century and a quarter still remain, silently, yet emphatically, reminding us of those whose voices are now hushed in death—occasional specimens—broken fragments and storm-beaten graves—the only mournful mementoes of the past.

Pre-eminent among these remains is the

INDIAN MOUND.

This peculiar method of perpetuating the memory, and of designating the last resting place of the departed, seems at a very early age to have suggested itself as the most natural and enduring. The Persians raised a mound at Aconithus over Artachies, the superintendent of the canal at Athos, which still exists, a memorial of Persian usage—a tribute to the memory of departed greatness—and a proof of the fidelity of Herodotus as a historian. Those mighty mounds that tower along the banks of the Borysthenes are the tombs of the Scythian kings, and that artificial hill near Sardis, in Asia Minor, that has braved the changing seasons for nearly twenty-five hundred years, is but the mound-tomb of Alyattes, king of Lydia.

Allusions to these structures are not unfrequent among the ancient poets. Thus Orestes, when addressing the manes of the murdered Agamemnon, says:

> "If but some Lycian spear 'neath Ilium's walls,
> Had lowly laid thee,
> A mighty name in the Atridan halls
> Thou wouldst have made thee!
> Then hadst thou pitched thy fortunes like a star,
> To son and daughter shining from afar!
> Beyond the wide-waved sea, *the high heaped mound*
> Had told forever
> Thy feats of battle, and with glory crowned
> Thy high endeavor."

A bare reference to Silbury Hill in Wiltshire, will call to remembrance that immense truncated cone, with its base of two thousand and twenty-seven feet, the sepulchral monument of the British King who founded the temple at Avebury. The vast plain of Salisbury,—"the most ancient and the most enigmatical of the reminiscences of England in the olden time"—is literally studded with tumuli, beneath which chieftains and priests have slept for centuries.

### LOCATION OF THE MOUNDS.

Although Indian mounds occur not unfrequently in almost every portion of Southern Georgia, they appear in greatest numbers upon the Sea-Islands. In choosing a location for them, respect seems universally to have been had to the natural advantages of the places selected. And as these mounds may be regarded as indicating the permanent seats and favorite resorts of the Indians, we are enabled to determine the localities at distant periods most thickly peopled by them.

As illustrations of the fact, that the mound was usually erected upon a spot possessing some natural advantages either for defense or for food, we may instance that large tumulus situated near the junction of Pipe Maker's creek and the Savannah River, or the mound which every one who has visited Darien must have observed on the neck of land, formed by the union of Cat-head creek and the Altamaha river.

On the Colonel's Island—lying between St. Catharine's and

the main—in the immediate vicinity of two copious natural springs, which, with generous undiminished flow have been sending forth their pure and refreshing waters for a period of time, whereof the memory of the white man runneth not to the the contrary—we have noticed no less than thirty or forty mounds, many of them quite prominent, with sharply defined outlines, while the action of the elements, and the oft-repeated furrows of the plough, render scarce perceptible the traces of others. In fact, this neighborhood may be aptly regarded as an *Indian Necropolis*.

Extended oyster beds—adjacent creeks filled with every variety of salt-water fish that frequents our coast—an island, in former years well stocked with game—in addition to the advantages afforded by a high and dry bluff—and the abundant supply of excellent fresh water—without doubt rendered this an uncommonly attractive spot to the Indian; and the remains here found, prove conclusively that the settlement must have been permanent and very general in its character.

It may be regarded as a fact that the Indian in forming a settlement, selected just the spot best suited to his convenience and comfort. As a further fact the deduction is both rational and necessary, that the mound was erected in the vicinity of his village or settlement, where the grave of a former chieftain, crafty in war, brave of heart, and wise in counsel, could ever remain in immediate view, to remind of an honored past, and to encourage to new attempts of valor—where the bones of fathers and family might repose in undisturbed security, watched over, guarded and visited by those, in whose veins coursed a kindred tide.

The wigwam, the council lodge, the rude building consecrated to sport and worship, even the evidences of agricultural pursuits have long since disappeared, and but for these mounds, all positive trace of their settlements would also in most instances have been lost.

### FORM AND SIZE OF THE MOUNDS.

In form, they are without exception, as far as our personal observation extends, *circular* and *conical*—sometimes a little *ovoidal*. There is every variety in size, from the large mound to which we have already alluded—situated on the Savannah river, near the junction of Pipe Maker's creek with that stream —which has a summit diameter of not less than fifty feet, and a diameter at the base of little less than one hundred, with an altitude of some twelve or fifteen feet, to the small shell mound, whose existence can scarcely be recognized. Many of them are almost level with the ground, and whitened bones mingled with fragments of pottery and implements of sport and warfare, lie exposed upon the very surface.

Composed as they are of the loose mould, and of the soft and yielding sand, they are extremely liable to diminution in size, and almost total obliteration. The consequence is, that they are all much reduced in size, and it is but reasonable to suppose, that many of the smaller ones, and those of oldest date have entirely disappeared. Human bones are not unfrequently found, where scarce a vestige of the mound can be perceived.

### ANTIQUITY OF THE MOUND.

In the absence of all historic information, the antiquity of the Indian mound would be readily inferred from its own internal evidence, as well as from the natural growth of the forest trees which completely overshadow it. One of the noblest specimens of the live-oak we have ever seen, grew upon the very summit, and with its majestic arms, threw a protecting shadow above and around the entire mound,—the dead, an untutored son of nature—his last resting place, a rude heap of native earth, in the solitude of the wild wood he once loved so well—his companions gone—his memory forgotten—and this pride of the forest, seemingly a guardian of the consecrated spot, with its deep foliage affording an inviting retreat wherein the pleasant birds of summer might warble their morning and evening songs—its sturdy roots protecting the symmetry of the grave—its over-arching boughs defending its yielding form from the ruthless influences of the tempest.

Attired in its garb of sober green—with its drapery of sombre moss swaying solemnly in the evening air, it appeared an aged, a heart felt mourner, watching over the dead of the children of the forest.

## USES OF THE MOUND.

A somewhat careful examination of several mounds leads us to the conclusion, that in this section of our State at least, they were used simply as places of sepulture. The general configuration, the uniformity of appearance, and their contents when ascertained, all tend to establish this fact. Nothing has fallen under our personal observation which would indicate, that they were ever designed as works of defense; nor have we any specimens of the Altaric or imitative mound, both of which occur not unfrequently in the West.

Notwithstanding this identity of form and unity of purpose, that may be traced in the mounds of Southern Georgia, they may admit of the following general classification.

## CLASSIFICATION OF MOUNDS.

First—The largest mounds containing but a single skeleton, we may for the purpose of convenience, designate as *Chieftain Mounds*.

Second.—Mounds of intermediate size filled with the remains of many dead, may be regarded as *Family or Tribal Mounds*.

Third—And lastly, we have the *Shell Mounds*, which differ from the Family or Tribal Mounds, simply in that they are generally much smaller, are completely covered with a layer of oyster, muscle and conch shells, and when opened, usually evince no traces of the action of fire.

## MOUNDS OF THE FIRST CLASS.

Those included under the first class are the most remarkable in size, and occupy the prominent or central position of the settlement. The human bones found in them indicate as a general rule, no action of fire. Nor do these mounds usually contain any charcoal, whose presence is very generally detected in the Family or Tribal Mounds. The skeleton is sometimes discovered in a sitting posture, and it is a matter of astonishment, in what a state of remarkable preservation the bones are, after the lapse of so many years.

Upon opening one of these mounds, it was quite evident that the body had been interred in a sitting posture—the elbows resting upon the knees,, and the hands supporting the chin. In the neighborhood of the ankles and wrists, were numerous bone-beads curiously fashioned, which, doubtless at the time of the inhumation, encircled the wrists, arms, and ankles. Near the pelvis, lay three stone axes, several spear-heads, two pipes of rather unusual size and form, and a bowl, doubtless the property of the deceased, which may have been deposited in his lap.

The fact that only a single skeleton is found in these mounds, and the further fact of their unusual size, very properly we think, designate them as the last resting places of the chiefs or distinguished personages of the tribe. Upon this supposition, we are enabled the more readily to understand the secret of their superior size. They may then be regarded as the results of the combined labors of the tribe or immediate community— each member with ready hand, assisting in erecting above and around the deceased leader, a mound, which, while it perpetuated the memory of the honored dead, and remained a monument of tribal respect, and tribal gratitude, begat also a pleasant satisfaction in the breast of every one who had assisted in its construction. Doubtless, each one of these now silent wasting mounds, has its legends transmitted from sire to son for generations—its heroic memories, that have brought the warm blood of conscious pride to the cheek alike of warrior and maiden; but these have all perished with those whose delight it was to perpetuate them, and memory will no more lift the shroud that time has cast over these buried recollections.

MOUNDS OF THE SECOND CLASS—BURNING THE DEAD.

It is a remarkable circumstance, and one which we have never seen noted, that it was a common custom among the Indians of Southern Georgia *to burn their dead.* We say a common custom, for our researches, while they establish the fact, also prove it not to have been universal. Those mounds which we include under the second class, almost always disclose when opened, charred human bones—and other proofs of the action of fire.

If we attempt to connect these mounds with many of a somewhat similar appearance in the West, it may be conjectured that they are Altaric in their character,—that the charcoal and the burnt earth indicate offerings by fire to the superior Deity,—that the pipes found within, are those with which the assembled worshippers made incense offerings to the Gods, and that when the ceremony was concluded, the pipes thus consecrated, were thrown into the smoking mass, and the loose earth heaped above to perpetuate the occasion and the rite.

But this inference is certainly without foundation, and for the simple reason, that in every mound in which is discovered the presence of fire, you will find human bones, charred and blackened, underlying and intermixed with this deposit of charcoal, half burnt pine-knots, and partially consumed portions of the ordinary woods of our section.

Our knowledge of Indian history teaches us, that this people never offered human sacrifices. What then is the plain inference? *Simply that the dead were burned.*

Nor were they singular in this custom. The ceremonies attending the Roman funeral—the pyra, the subsequent urning of the ashes, are as familiar to every one, as the testified and holy horror of the ancient Christians, to the Pagan custom of burning the dead.

The peculiar funeral rites of the Indians, cannot now of course be definitely ascertained, but there are certain general features disclosed upon an examination of the constitution and contents of the mounds.

The corpse or skeleton, with a requisite amount of wood, was first laid upon the level earth. Fire was applied, and above the smouldering remains the mass of earth heaped, which we denominate an Indian mound. The charred bones and burnt wood are never seen, until you have reached, or very nearly so, the level of the plain. The body then having been burnt upon the ground, and no care having been bestowed in the subsequent arrangement of the half consumed skeleton, the mound was all an after work. As we have already intimated, this custom of burning the dead was not universal. Why it should have been adopted in some instances, and not in others, must remain a matter only for conjecture.

If the mound then be the result of the combined labor of the many, exerted at one and the same time,—if it be true that the dead were first laid upon the ground, and the earth subsequently heaped above,—if the dead were burned upon the very spot upon which the mound now stands; if it be also the fact, that the overlying stratum of charred wood appears uniform and unbroken, the question naturally suggests itself, how happens it that there are the remains of many skeletons in a single mound? The conformation, the internal evidence, the theory of mound-building, all forbid the supposition that when once completed, they were ever afterwards reopened for the purpose of receiving new bodies. Are we to regard them simply as the common receptacles of the dead of the battlefield?

Bartram noticed among the Choctaws the following funeral custom:—

As soon as a person is dead, they erect a scaffold some eighteen or twenty feet high, in a grove adjacent to the town, where they lay the corpse lightly covered with a mantle: here it is suffered to remain, visited and protected by the friends and relations, until the flesh becomes putrid, so as easily to part from the bones; then, undertakers, who make it their business, carefully strip the flesh from the bones, wash and cleanse them, and when dry and purified by the air, having provided a curiously wrought chest or coffin, fabricated of bones and splints, they place all the bones therein,—it is then deposited in the bone-house, a building erected for that purpose, in every town. And when this house is full, a general solemn funeral takes place. The nearest kindred or friends of the deceased, on a day appointed, repair to the bone-house, take up the respective coffins, and following one another in the order of seniority, the nearest relations and connexions attending their respective corpse, and the multitude following after them, all as one family, with united voice of alternate Allelujah, and lamentation, proceed to the place of general interment, where they place the coffins in order, forming a pyramid, and lastly cover all over with earth, which raises a conical hill or mount.

Mr. Jefferson, (notes on Virginia, query XI,) examined with much care, a Barrow on the low grounds of the Rivanna, about two miles above its principal fork, and opposite to some hills on which had been an Indian town. He found it to be a repository of the dead, and conjectured that it contained a thousand skeletons.

He says: Appearances certainly indicate that it (the Barrow) derived both origin and growth from the accustomary collection of bones, and deposition of them together: that the first collection had been deposited on the common surface of the earth—a few stones put over it, and then a covering of earth; that the second had been laid on this, had covered more or less of it in proportion to the number of bones, and was covered with earth, and so on.

In this barrow, the bones lay in strata, entirely separated by intervening spaces of earth, the bones themselves indicating the fact, that they had lain for different periods in the earth, those nearest the surface being least decayed.

That the Indians of Southern Georgia must have adopted the custom of *reserving* the bodies or skeletons of the dead, until they had accumulated sufficiently, to *warrant a general burning and a general inhumation*, seems an inference fairly to be deduced from the appearance and contents of the mounds. The solitary dead may sleep in an unknown grave, but the mound covers the many, is a public tomb, the product of the combined labors of a community.

It was no easy task for the aborigines to erect a tumulus. Under the most favorable circumstances, it must have proved a slow, severe, and onerous undertaking.

The mounds in Southern Georgia, so far as we have examined them, contain but a single stratum of bones, and that, *even with* the surface of the ground; showing, that when the inhumation was over, and the tumulus heaped above, it was never again re-opened to receive new bodies. The bones themselves lie without order; as a general rule, in the utmost confusion, some vertical, some oblique, some horizontal, the effect doubtless of the careless gathering together of the partially consumed remains, previous to the erection of the mound above.

SHELL MOUNDS.

The shell mound is the smallest of the mounds, and occurs most frequently. On the coast, it appears to have been the common grave of the Indian. The fields now under cultivation on the islands, are filled with them;—each one exhibiting the remains of many skeletons; but among those which we have examined, we find but few indicating the action of fire. The probability is, that they were covered with this layer of oyster shells, to give permanency to the tumulus, which being quite small, would otherwise have been liable to early obliteration.

In opening one of this class, intermingled with the human bones, was seen a portion of the skeleton of a dog. Are we to understand from this circumstance, that the Indian permitted this faithful and attached companion, who, with an untiring devotion had followed the footsteps of his owner through the trackless forest, assisting by day in the active pursuit, and when night drew her sable curtains around the sleeper, with ceaseless vigil warned him of the coming danger, to enjoy in death *an equal funeral rite, and a common grave with his master and friend ?*

### FUNERAL VASES.

The use of funeral vases was not uncommon among the Indians. The one which we have before us, was found on the Colonels Island, some eighteen inches below the surface, in a small shell mound. It was the innermost of three. The two exterior vases, acted upon more immediately by the moisture of the earth, in which they had lain for certainly a century and a quarter, (and how much longer, who can tell?) were in a yielding and fractured condition. When lifted from their position, they fell in pieces; completely covering the top of the exterior vase, was a lid or cap of the same material, closely fitting. This removed, within the smallest vase thus protected, was the frail skeleton of an infant. Placed there perchance, by some affectionate mother, with the fond hope that this rude clay coffin, her own handiwork, would shield the tender form she loved so well, from the chilling damp, and the remorseless decay of the silent tomb—affecting exhibition of that sincere natural attachment for her offspring, which not death itself can teach even the uncivilized parent to forget. Other instances of a similar character have fallen under our observation.

## CUSTOM OF BURYING IMPLEMENTS, UTENSILS, &c., WITH THE DEAD.

That the Indians of our section adopted the custom, so general in almost every portion of this continent, of interring with the deceased, their ornaments, and implements of toil, sport and warfare, is abundantly proved by the numbers of stone tomahawks, axes, knives, pots, pipes, beads, arrow and spear heads, contained in the mounds.

The peculiar religious belief in which this custom finds its warrant, is familiar to us all. In a recent communication to Hiawatha, from the inmates of the spirit land, it appears however, that it has become a grevious one to the weary travellers, and through him they entreat their countrymen not to

> "—— lay such heavy burdens
> In the graves of those they bury.
> Not such weight of furs and wampum,
> Not such weight of pots and kettles,
> For the spirits faint beneath them.
> Only give them food to carry,
> Only give them fire to light them."

### INDIANS OF SOUTHERN GEORGIA NOT IDOLATERS.

Of the religious rites of the Indians, we find no positive monumental traces. Whatever may have been their objects of worship, they have left, so far as we have been able to ascertain, not even a rude clay Idol.

With them, the great spirit dwelt not in temples made with hands. The deep, the boundless, the trackless forest was his hunting ground—the blue heavens, his home—the stars, his lamps—the deep toned thunder, his voice of anger—the softly breathing winds of evening, his kindly whisper. Like the ancient Germans, the Indians of Southern Georgia did not consider it in accordance with the greatness, or the dignity of celestial beings to confine them within walls, or to liken them to the human form, or fashion them after the image of beast, or bird.

### BEADS.

From some mounds, hundreds of beads have been taken. Of these there are three varieties—(a)

The *bead of silex*, or of some stone capable of receiving a high degree of polish—oval, or elliptical in shape, with a hole neatly drilled through the centre in the direction of the major axis.—(b)

*The ordinary clay bead*, fashioned after the same model, but of course much ruder, and less attractive in its appearance, the ornament having been formed when the clay was soft and plastic in its character, and subsequently hardened by subjecting it, sometimes to the heat of the fire, at other times, simply the influence of the sun's rays, and lastly—(c)

We find the *bone bead*, the most readily made of them all, and the smallest,—often not more than a quarter of an inch in length. Nature having already furnished convenient material in the wing bone of a bird—the vertebra of a fish, or the radius of a small animal, all that was requisite for the final completion of the bead was, that it be cut of the required length, and prepared with the necessary polish.

The ingenuity and skill displayed in forming the stone bead, become the more remarkable when we recollect, that they were fashioned in their present symmetry of outline and accuracy of proportion, without the assistance of a single iron file, or an ordinary drill.

STONE TOMAHAWK AND HATCHET.

Of their weapons of warfare, and daily use, the stone tomahawk and the axe are not unworthy a moments notice. The tomahawk is not unfrequently ten inches or more in length. The specimen before us, was found only a few months since in a newly cleared field. It now bears the scar, made by a spade used in opening a drain. To have fastened it to a handle, they must have split the wood, placed the small end of the tomahawk in the opening, then brought the split ends together and lashed them securely with a thong of some sort, or more likely with deer sinews. The use of the sinew, is said to have been very generally adopted by the Indian. Those of us who have not forgotten the sports of boy-hood's days, will remember with pleasure, how admirably adapted it was for seasoning the feather to the arrow.

The second specimen is a small hatchet, double-edged, with a hole drilled through the centre. Into this, the handle could very conveniently have been introduced. Many hatchets are destitute of this drill, but frequently have a groove, by means o fwhich the handle could be secured. Others still, want both drill and groove.

I once asked an Indian in upper Georgia, in what manner a hatchet of this latter discription was fastened to a handle. His reply was, that it was sometimes secured with sinews, and at other times, a small growing tree was split while standing, and into the slit the hatchet introduced, and allowed there to remain until the wood gradually closed around it, when a handle was cut of the proper length, smoothed, and ornamented to suit the taste of the owner. This however, being necessarily a slow process, could not have been generally adopted.

The shape of the tomahawk and the axe would seem to indicate, that they were designed rather as weapons of warfare, than as implements of toil. It is a known fact, that the Indian on almost every occasion called in fire to his assistance. Through its intervention, the tree selected for the future canoe was felled, and burnt off at the required distances. Through its agency, the sides were rudely fashioned, and the inner portion hollowed out. It is not improbable, that these hatchets were employed in removing the charred surface, and in giving a finish to the work; but for actual hewing or accurate chopping, they must have proved entirely useless.

### SPEAR AND ARROW-HEADS.

Of all the remains which still exist, silently reminding us of the almost forgotten Indian, none are so abundant as the spear, and the arrow-heads. These lie scattered in every wood, in every field—wrought with surprising symmetry and beauty, they are speaking commentaries on the skill and proficiency of those by whom they were chipped.

The form of the dart is familiar to us all, and we can but admire the adaptation of means to an end, displayed in their shape and construction.

We have before us, six modifications of the one general idea. Fearful must have been the wound inflicted, and difficult the extraction of one of these arrow heads, when it had completely buried itself in the quivering flesh. Some of them have serrated edges, rendering still more dangerous the received wound.

The largest without doubt were weapons of war—those of a medium size were used in the chase, and in spearing fish, while the smallest sufficed to bring down the wild turkey, the squirrel, and other small game. To them, reeds or handles were secured with sinews, the end split receiving the arrow, or spear-head, the sinew passing around and through the space between the wings and the handle of the dart, and thus binding the point and shaft securely together. We have occasionally seen a specimen, which could have been readily introduced into the hollow end of a reed, after the manner of a spike.

The ingenuity and skill displayed in the construction of these darts, become the more surprising, when we remember, that their well chipt proportions were attained, simply with the assistance of a rude stone chisel. The inquiry naturally suggests itself, where did the Indians obtain these spear and arrow heads? We have neither silex nor quartz rock in the southern portion of our State, and scarcely in the middle sections can suitable material be conveniently obtained. We remember to have read—but where, we cannot now positively recollect—that among the Indians who inhabited the mountains, there was a certain number or class, who devoted their time and attention to the manufacture of these darts. That as soon as they had prepared a general supply, they left their mountain homes, and visited the sea-board and intermediate localities, exchanging their spear and arrow heads, for other articles not to be readily obtained in the region where they inhabited. The further fact was stated, that these persons never mingled in the excitements of war—that to them a free passport was at all times granted, even among tribes actually at variance with that of which they were members—that their avocation was esteemed honorable, and they themselves treated with universal hospitality. If such was the case, it was surely a remarkable and interesting recognition of the claims of the manufacturer, by an untutored race.

Be this as it may, there are certainly not a few indications —sufficient we think to establish the fact—that the Indians of Southern Georgia, often manufactured at home, their own arrow and spear heads, and probably all the stone utensils employed by them. Often is a rude mass of silex found in the field, or in the neighborhood of one of their ancient settlements, brought without doubt from a distance, and preserved to be used and worked up as occasion and necessity required. There are moreover, half finished arrow heads—cast aside on account of some inherent defect in the stone, of which they were forming them; and occasionally are seen places covered with broken darts, and numerous chips struck from the stone in the construction of the spear and arrow heads—thus conclusively proving, that at least these weapons of sport and warfare, were *here manufactured* by the Indians. We have in our possession a number of these chips, and half formed darts.

### POTS, PANS, &C.

William Bartram, who visited this State in 1778, under the auspices of Dr. Fothergill of London, while upon the Colonels Island, opposite Sunbury, in Liberty County, observed among the shells of the conical mounds, fragments of earthen vessels, and of other utensils, the manufacture of the ancients. About the centre (he writes) of one of these, the rim of an earthen pot appeared amongst the shells and earth, which I carefully removed, and drew it out almost whole; this pot was curiously wrought all over, the outside representing basket work, and was undoubtedly esteemed a very ingenious performance by the people at the age of its construction.

It is a singular coincidence, and one perhaps not unworthy of note, that the funeral vase now before us, was found upon the same Island, and under circumstances precisely similar to those described by Mr. Bartram. A simple glance at its form and general appearance, will attest the accuracy of the old travellers observation and description.

Broken pieces of pottery lie mingled with the leaves of our forests, and are seen scattered every where in our fields—especially do they abound upon our sea islands, the numerous fragments proving conclusively, the general use among the Indians of the pot, the pan, the bowl and the funeral vase.

Composed as they are of clay and gravel, in consequence of the frail character of the vessel formed of this material, it is now a very rare occurrence to obtain one of them in a perfect condition. Time and the changing seasons, have in most instances robbed them of their original symmetry, and only broken fragments remain, to remind us of their former shape and size. The accuracy of form, and we may add beauty of outline, are often remarkable. The bowls are generally quite plain, with simply an ornamented rim, while the larger pots and vases, bear the impress of various and often ingenious designs.

One method adopted in the manufacture of these last, appears to have been this: a basket of the desired size, shape and design, was first made of rushes or split oak—the meshes arranged to suit the taste, and ingenuity of the potter. Within this, the clay, in a soft adhesive state, was then spread of the desired thickness, conforming of course to the exact form of the basket work by which it was thus surrounded—suffered to remain in this condition until the clay became hard and dry, the reed or basket-work was then removed, the pot or vase retaining its shape and identity, and the impressions which we now observe, permanently established. Doubtless, in many instances these articles were subjected to the further process of hardening by fire. The rims are often highly ornamented with impressions of various kinds.

In perhaps not a few instances, the pots and vases were fashioned without the assistance of this basket work; the vessel being moulded by the hand, and the figures on the outside, made while the clay was still soft, with bone awls, rude stamps, &c. Very many of their ordinary pots, bowls and pans, are perfectly plain, both within and without. These common articles seem to have been prepared with apparently little care.

Especially within and about the shell mounds, do we find the most numerous specimens of the ornamental funeral vase. The remains are however, in almost every instance, quite fragmentary in their character.

If the enduring marble, after the lapse of many years, loses its polish, and often ceases entirely to reflect the life and love, which irradiated its pure form, when first it came, instinct with grace and beauty from the studio of the sculptor, can we wonder that these frail earthen vessels, should have yielded to the disintegrating influences of the suns and storms of centuries?

It was the observation of Mr. Bartram, that all the pottery used by the Indians, was manufactured by the women—the men with one consent delegating this to the females. Busied with the excitements of the chase and the ambush, they had neither time nor inclination for this earth-born, tedious, manual occupation.

PIPES AND CALUMETS.

The pipe is said to have been regarded by the Indians, with feelings of peculiar fondness and veneration. A pleasant companion amid the loneliness of the forest, its presence was always welcome when the friendly circle gathered around the wigwam fire. The Council Lodge too, was filled with the perfumed clouds that slowly ascended from its ample bowl. In testimony of the consummation of an alliance—upon a declaration of war—or the confirmation of a treaty of peace—its aid was deemed indispensable in the solemn ratification of the act. A whiff from the calumet, was then the signing and sealing by the parties in interest. When the tomahawk was buried, it became the token of peace and good will—when the hatchet was lifted, it was among brothers the most solemn pledge of mutual confidence, and mutual devotion to the interests of their common cause.

To us of the present day, the old Indian pipe, with its broken bowl and defaced image, is invested with a peculiar attraction.

Those of the ordinary class, found in tribal and shell mounds, and picked up not unfrequently in the fields, are made of common clay, some of them very rudely and plainly constructed, others fashioned with no inconsiderable symmetry. The human countenance, with distorted features and tattooed cheek, is in some instances delineated upon the front of the bowl. They are without stems—the inserted reeds having long since mingled their dust, with the earth of the mound tomb, or of the wood.

We occasionally meet with a pipe made of soap stone, but specimens of this description are very rare, those in common use among the Indians being formed simply of the red or blue clay, so abundant in this region. The pipes however, most remarkable in size, and most worthy of attention, are the *Calumets*.

These, as might reasonably be supposed, are very rare. The specimen before us, was taken from a large chieftain mound in McIntosh County. We have called it a calumet, because its size and peculiar conformation seem to forbid the supposition, that it generally attended the person of the owner, or was used ordinarily by any one member of the tribe. The flattened surface of the bottom, its weight, and unusual size, would indicate the fact that it must have rested upon the ground, while the size of the aperture for the stem, suggests the use of a reed of no ordinary length. Knowing the customs of the Indians, we incline to the belief, that this was indeed one of their esteemed calumets, regarded in times past with emotions near akin to veneration, and only used upon occasions of no ordinary interest and moment.

How simple, and yet how impressive, the ceremony of smoking the pipe of peace! How emblematic this silent rite of the calm that succeeds the storm, of the quiet repose that reigned within the breasts, of late heaving so madly with the wild excitements of war and bloody hate! How much more appropriate this method of pledging a restoration of mutual confidence, friendship and faith, than that, adopted by the bloodthirsty followers of Odin!

The many ornaments with which they were wont to be decorated, the long tapering stems, adorned with eagle plumes, are no more seen, and the naked pipe remains, a mournful memento of an almost lost race, and of a ceremony in itself unique, one which the Indian always regarded with especial pride and honor.

But we have already in this hurried sketch, trespassed too largely upon the indulgence of this audience, to bestow even a passing notice upon the stone-mortars and pestles, the round flat paint and grinding stones—the stones used in dressing the deer-skin—the fleshing knife, the bone-awl, and minor utensils of a similar character.

Fashioned all in the same rude manner, they but scarcely answered the purposes for which they were designed by the unskilled aborigines, and are now prized only by the antiquary, as in lonely places he seeks for some memorial of a neglected past.

The sorrowing circle will never again assemble around the funeral fires, nor stalwart arms, above the ashes of the dead, heap the rude mound-tomb. Never more will a weeping mother, with trembling hand, fashion the funeral vase. The eagle-eye that gave unerring aim to the pointed shaft, has looked for the last time upon forest and river. Like summer clouds, the forms of warrior and maiden have passed away. The intrepid Brave no more bends his ear to the voice of the storm God, as he speaks in the deep-toned thunder, and beneath the pale moon-beams, we seek in vain for the images of the loving and the loved.

> "Alas! for them, their day is o'er,
> Their fires are out from shore to shore;
> No more for them the wild deer bounds,
> The plough is on their hunting grounds,
> The pale man's axe rings thro' their woods,
> The pale man's sail skims o'er their floods,
> Their pleasant springs are dry."

Upon this occasion, Gentlemen of the Georgia Historical Society—your anniversary—an occasion, graced as it is by the presence of intelligence and beauty, it may have been expected that we should have selected some theme, nobler than that which has this evening invited your attention—a theme, whose discussion would have presented much that is entertaining, much that is exalted in the history of our State and nation. And who that reflects but for one moment, can fail of finding subjects replete with the deepest interest, whether we lend a listening ear to the voices of the past, as they speak of the early struggles of an infant colony, as they remind us of the subsequent advancement, and the present enviable position which our country occupies in the Republic of Letters, of Art, or of Invention;—whether we consult the heroic records of our Revolutionary period, illustrative as they are, of all that is pure in principle, wonderful in conception, noble in action, and stupendous in result; or mark the triumphs of Peace, as she spreads her white wings over a land smiling in plenty, and rejoicing in the benign influences of her happy reign. Over this very City, the hostile cannon once

> "Pealed its hoarsest strains,"

and the war-cloud descended in all its fury. In our very streets, the contest for freedom was fought. The blood, the sacred blood of our forefathers, still calls to us from the very soil which we tread, in tones of moving eloquence, "my sons, forget not your fathers." And we should not—we do not, and by all that is sacred in the past, we will not forget them.

Already have monuments been erected in the high places of our beautiful Savannah, to the memory of the brave departed, who interposed their stout hearts and strong arms, in the support and prosecution of the early struggle for independence.

When the hands that reared them are motionless, when the hearts, that now beat so high at mention of their names, at thought of their generous heroic efforts, shall have ceased their wonted action, "the graven stone shall bear witness to other ages of our gratitude, and their worth. And ages still further on, when the monuments themselves like those who built them, shall have crumbled to dust, the happy aspect of the land which our fathers redeemed, shall remain one common, one eternal monument to their memory."

In the breast of every "good and true" citizen, is erected an altar, consecrated to the worship of all that is excellent, all that is ennobling in the history of his State and country;—an altar, from whose vestal fires is ever ascending, the incense of gratitude for the past, honor for the present, and fervent prayer for the unsullied prosperity of the future.

With such memories clustering thickly about your every pathway, it needs not, Gentlemen, that you should now be reminded of their presence, or be entreated to preserve and cherish every object illustrative of their influences, and of the history of the great men, and the consecrated spots, that give to them such dignity and worth.

Turning aside from the delightful contemplation of such inviting, soul-stirring themes, we have presented for your notice, a few decaying memorials of a Race, intimately associated with the first settlement of Georgia. And surely, in the eyes of those, self-charged with the preservation of everything connected with the early history and antiquities of our State, they cannot prove uninteresting or valueless.

In this view, it may not repent us, that we have devoted one hour to staying the ruthless waves of time, as they are fast effacing the last footprints of a neglected race;—that we have paused for one moment, to shed a tear of heartfelt sympathy upon the grave, the lonely, the storm-beaten grave of the almost forgotten Indian.

Printed by Libri Plureos GmbH in Hamburg, Germany